Active Directory
Fast Start

Smart Brain Training Solutions

Thank you for purchasing *Active Directory Fast Start*! We hope you'll look for other *Fast Start* guides from Smart Brain Training Solutions.

Table of Contents

1. Introduction

Active Directory is an extensible directory service that enables centralized management of network resources. It allows you to easily add, remove, or relocate accounts for users, groups, and computers as well as other types of resources. Nearly every administrative task you perform affects Active Directory in some way. Active Directory is based on standard Internet protocols and has a design that helps you clearly identify the physical and logical components of your network's structure.

Active Directory provides the necessary infrastructure for designing a directory that meets the needs of your organization. A *directory* is a stored collection of information about various types of resources. In a distributed computing environment such as a Windows network, users must be able to locate and use distributed resources, and administrators must be able to manage how distributed resources are used. This is why a directory service is necessary.

A *directory service* stores all the information needed to use and manage distributed resources in a centralized location. The service makes it possible for resources to work together. It is responsible for authorizing access, managing identities, and controlling the relationships between the resources. Because a directory service provides these fundamental functions, it must be tightly integrated with the security and management features of the network operating system.

A directory service provides the means to define and maintain the network infrastructure, perform system administration, and control the user experience. Although users and administrators might not know the exact resources they need, they should know some basic characteristics of the resources they want to use. If so, they can use the directory service to obtain a list of resources that match the known characteristics. As illustrated in Figure 1, they can use the directory service to query the directory and locate resources that have specific characteristics. For example, users can search the directory to find a color printer in a particular location or to find a color printer that supports duplex functionality.

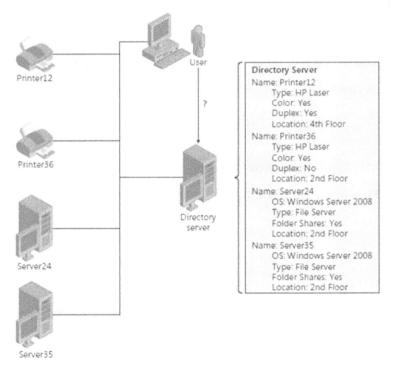

Figure 1 Working with directory services.

Because a directory service is a tool for both administrators and standard users, administrators can also use the directory to locate resources. For example, an administrator could locate file servers running Windows Server 2012 R2. As an organization grows and its network grows with it, there are more and more resources to manage, and the directory service becomes increasingly important.

2. Working with Active Directory

Active Directory is the directory service included with Windows Server. Active Directory includes the directory that stores information about your distributed resources as well as the services that make the information useful and available. All current versions of Windows Server support Active Directory.

Active Directory Domains

Windows domains that use Active Directory are called *Active Directory domains*. In an Active Directory domain, your data resides in a single, distributed data repository that requires less administration to maintain while also allowing easy access from any location on the network. Using the physical and logical structures provided by Active Directory, you can scale the directory to meet your business and network requirements whether you have hundreds, thousands, or millions of resources.

Active Directory is designed to interoperate with other directory services and to accept requests from many different clients using a variety of interfaces, as shown in Figure 2. The primary protocol Active Directory uses is Lightweight Directory Access Protocol (LDAP) version 3, an industry-standard protocol for directory services. When working with other Windows servers, Active Directory supports replication through the REPL interface. When working with legacy messaging clients, Active Directory supports Messaging Application Programming Interface (MAPI). Active Directory also supports the Security Accounts Manager (SAM) interface.

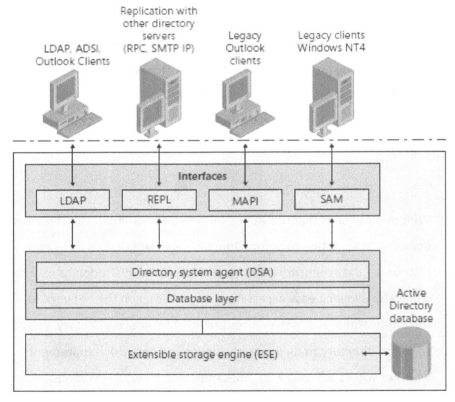

Figure 2 Active Directory can interoperate with clients and other directory services.

Active Directory authentication and authorization services use Kerberos version 5 and other industry-standard protocols to provide protection for data by default while maximizing flexibility. For example, by default Active Directory signs and encrypts all communications that use LDAP. Signing LDAP communications ensures data comes from a known source and has not been modified.

Active Directory is integrated with Windows Server security. As with files and folders, you can control access to distributed resources in the directory by using a granular set of permissions. You also can control access to the properties of distributed resources. Additionally, Active Directory provides security groups for administration at various levels throughout the enterprise.

In Active Directory, group policies are used to define permitted actions and settings for users and computers. Policy-based management simplifies many administration tasks. Group policies can be applied in many different ways. One way is to use security templates to configure the initial security of a computer.

DNS Domains

Active Directory uses the Domain Name System (DNS). DNS is a standard Internet service that organizes groups into a hierarchical structure. Although implemented for different reasons, Active Directory and DNS have the same hierarchical structure. The DNS hierarchy is defined on an Internet-wide basis for public networks and an enterprise-wide basis for private networks. The various levels within the DNS hierarchy identify individual computers and the relationship between computers. The relationship between computers is expressed by using domains. Computers that are part of the same DNS domain are closely related. Domains used within organizations are *organizational domains*. Domains at the root of the DNS hierarchy are *top-level,* or *root,* domains.

Active Directory clients use DNS to locate resources. DNS translates easily readable host names to numeric Internet Protocol (IP) addresses. Each computer in a domain has a fully qualified domain name (FQDN), such as server34.microsoft.com. Here, *server34* represents the name of an individual computer, *microsoft* represents the organizational domain, and *com* is the top-level domain.

Top-level domains (TLDs) are at the base of the DNS hierarchy. TLDs are organized geographically by using two-letter country codes, such as *CA* for Canada; by organization type, using codes such as *com* for commercial organizations; and by function, using codes such as *mil* for U.S. military installations.

Like top-level domains, DNS domains within an organization can be structured in many ways. Normal domains, such as microsoft.com, are also referred to as parent domains. They have this name because they're the parents of an organizational structure. You can divide parent domains into subdomains, which you can then use for different offices, divisions, or geographic locations. For example, the FQDN for a computer at City Power & Light's Denver office could be designated as workstation11.denver.imaginedlands.com. Here, *workstation11* is the computer name, *denver* is the subdomain, and *imaginedlands.com* is the parent domain. Another term for a subdomain is *child domain.*

Updates to DNS are handled through a single authoritative DNS server. This server is designated as the primary DNS server for the particular domain or area within a domain called the *zone*. The primary DNS server stores a master copy of DNS records and a domain's configuration files. Secondary DNS servers provide additional services for a domain to help balance the workload. Secondary servers store copies of DNS records obtained from a primary server through a process called a *zone transfer*. Secondary servers obtain their DNS information from a primary server when they're started, and they maintain this information until the information is refreshed or expired.

In Figure 3, the primary DNS server is responsible for DNS domains imaginedlands.com, data.imaginedlands.com, and recs.imaginedlands.com. Secondary DNS servers in the data.imaginedlands.com and recs.imaginedlands.com domains obtain their DNS information from this primary server through periodic zone transfers.

Active Directory depends so much on DNS that you should either configure DNS on the network before you install Active Directory or allow the Active Directory Installation wizard to install DNS for you. Configuring DNS requires installing and configuring DNS clients and DNS servers. All Windows operating systems include DNS clients and can be configured with fully qualified host names. Any computer running the Windows Server operating system can be configured as a DNS server.

When you configure Active Directory on your network, you can automatically install DNS as part of Active Directory installation. You can also specify whether DNS and Active Directory should be integrated partially or fully. As integration with Active Directory changes the way DNS works, understanding the integration options is very important.

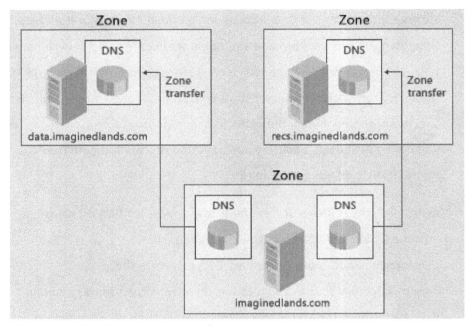

Figure 3 A DNS environment with zones.

With partial integration, the domain uses standard file storage, and updates to DNS are handled exactly as discussed previously. The domain has a single primary server and one or more secondary DNS servers. Secondary DNS servers obtain their DNS information from the primary DNS server.

With full integration, DNS information is stored directly in Active Directory. Because the information is part of Active Directory, you gain all the benefits of Active Directory and your domain uses Active Directory to update and maintain DNS information.

Domain Controllers

When you install Windows Server on a computer, you can configure the computer as a stand-alone server, a member server, or a domain controller. A *domain controller* (DC) is a computer that hosts an Active Directory directory. You install Active Directory in two steps. First you add the Active Directory Domain Services role to the server by using the Add Role Wizard. Then you run the Active Directory Installation Wizard. If DNS isn't installed already, you are prompted to install DNS. If there isn't an existing domain, the wizard helps you create a domain and configure Active Directory in the new domain. The wizard can also help you add child domains to existing domain structures.

> **Note**   Unlike earlier releases of Windows Server, Windows Server 2008 R2, Windows Server 2012 and later only run on 64-bit hardware.

Unlike early Windows Server operating systems, current versions of Windows Server do not designate primary or backup domain controllers. Instead, Windows Server supports a multimaster replication model. In this model, as shown in Figure 4, any domain controller can process directory changes and then replicate those changes to other domain controllers automatically.

This differs from the Windows NT single-master replication model, in which the primary domain controller stores a master copy and backup controllers store backup copies of the master. In addition, Windows NT distributed only the Security Accounts Manager (SAM) database, but current releases of Windows Server distribute the entire directory of information regarding distributed resources.

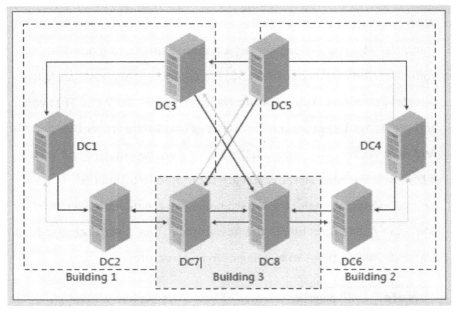

Figure 4 Any domain controller can replicate changes.

Real World   Because some changes are impractical to perform in multimaster fashion, Active Directory also uses single-master replication. Here, one or more domain controllers, designated as operations masters, are assigned to perform operations that are not permitted to occur at different places on the network at the same time.

Active Directory uses a multimaster approach to provide many performance and availability benefits. Multimaster replication allows you to update the directory at any domain controller. That domain controller in turn replicates the changes to other domain controllers. When you have multiple domain controllers deployed, replication continues even if any single domain controller fails.

Although Active Directory domains can function with only one domain controller, you can and should configure multiple domain controllers in your domains. This way, if one domain controller fails, you can rely on another domain controller to handle authentication and other critical tasks.

Domain controllers manage all aspects of a user's interaction with Active Directory domains. They validate user logon attempts, locate objects, and much more. Within Active Directory, directory information is logically partitioned. Each domain controller stores a copy of all pertinent partitions. The pertinent partitions for a particular domain controller are determined by where the domain controller is located and how the domain controller is used.

Domain controllers manage changes for information they store and replicate changes to other domain controllers as appropriate. Because of how replication works, a conflict can occur if an attribute is modified on a domain controller, because a change to the same attribute on another domain controller is propagated. Active Directory resolves the conflict by comparing each attribute's property version number (a value initialized when an attribute is created and updated each time an attribute is changed) and replicating the changed attribute with the higher property version number.

Normally domain controllers are readable and writable. However, Windows Server 2008, Windows Server 2008 R2, Windows Server 2012 and later also support read-only domain controllers. A *read-only domain controller* (RODC) is a domain controller that hosts a read-only replica of a domain's directory. By default, RODCs store no passwords or credentials besides those used for their own computer account and the Kerberos Target (krbtgt) account. This makes RODCs ideal for branch offices where a domain controller's physical security cannot be guaranteed.

Figure 5 shows an RODC deployed to a branch office. Here the main office has multiple domain controllers with writable data. The branch office has an RODC with read-only data. The RODC is placed at the branch office because the physical security of the server cannot be guaranteed.

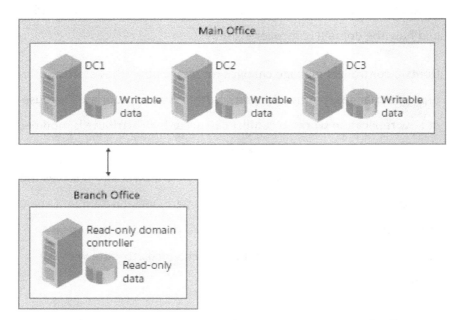

Figure 5 A read-only domain controller deployed to a branch office.

Tip Except for passwords, RODCs store the same objects and attributes as writable domain controllers. These objects and attributes are replicated to RODCs by using unidirectional replication from a writable domain controller that acts as a replication partner. Although RODCs can pull information from domain controllers running Windows Server 2003, RODCs can pull updates of the domain partition only from a writable domain controller running Windows Server 2008 or later in the same domain.

RODCs pull user and computer credentials from a writable domain controller running Windows Server 2008 or later. Then, if allowed by the Password Replication Policy that is enforced on the writable domain controller, RODCs cache credentials as necessary until the credentials change. Because only subsets of credentials are stored on RODCs, the credentials that can possibly be compromised are limited.

3. Active Directory Objects

Resources that you want to represent in Active Directory are created and stored as objects. Objects have attributes that define the kinds of information you want to store about resources. For example, the User object in Active Directory has attributes that help describe users, including first name, middle initial, last name, and display name. The Computer object in Active Directory has attributes that help describe computers, such as the computer's name, description, location, and security identifier.

Objects in the directory are either leaf objects or container objects. Objects that can't contain other objects are *leaf objects,* or simply *leafs.* Objects that hold other objects are referred to as *container objects,* or simply *containers*. The directory itself is a container that contains other containers and objects. In Figure 6, the Users object is a container that contains User objects, the Computers object is a container that contains Computer objects, and the Printers object is a container that contains Printer objects.

Each object created within the directory is of a particular class. The Active Directory schema defines the available object classes and provides rules that determine how you can create and use objects. Available object classes include User, Group, Computer, and Printer.

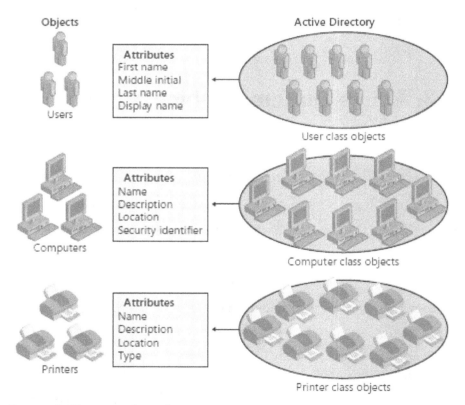

Figure 6 Objects and attributes in Active Directory.

Active Directory Schema

Essentially, the *schema* is a list of definitions that determines object classes and the types of information about the object classes that can be stored in the directory. The schema definitions themselves are stored as one of two types of objects:

- Schema class objects, or simply schema classes
- Schema attribute objects, or simply schema attributes

As shown in Figure 7, schema class objects and attribute objects are defined separately in the directory. You can refer to both sets of objects collectively as *schema objects.*

Schema class objects describe the objects you can create. They function as templates for creating new objects. Within a particular schema class, the schema attributes store the information that describes related objects. For example, the User, Group, Computer, and Printer classes are composed of many schema attributes. The User class has attributes that describe users. The Group class has attributes that describe groups of users. The Computer class has attributes that describe computers. The Printer class has attributes that describe printers.

> **Tip** Each schema attribute is defined only once and can be used in multiple schema classes. For example, the Description attribute is defined only once in the schema but is used in the User, Group, Computer, and Printer classes as well as other classes.

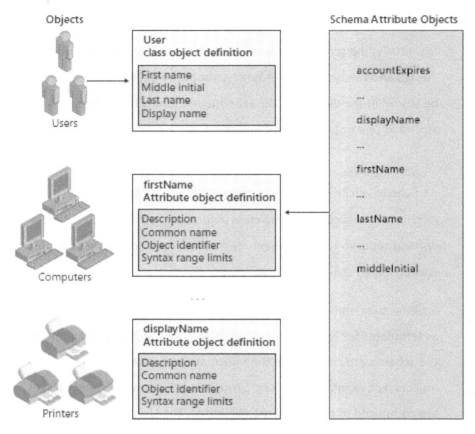

Figure 7 Objects within a schema.

A core set of schema classes and attributes is included with Active Directory. Because the directory is extensible, other application and server products can dynamically extend the schema. For example, when you install Microsoft Exchange Server in the enterprise, Exchange Server extension classes and attributes are added to the directory. Any new extensions to the directory are replicated automatically as appropriate.

> **Note** Experienced developers and administrators can extend the schema as well. However, extending the schema is an advanced procedure that should be planned and tested carefully before it is implemented. Also, keep in mind that once defined, the extended schema classes and attributes can be deactivated but cannot be deleted. You cannot deactivate or delete schema objects that are part of the default schema that ships with Active Directory.

Active Directory Components

You can use a variety of Active Directory components to define the structure of the directory. These components are organized into physical and logical layers. Physical layer components control how directory information is structured and stored. Logical layer components control how users and administrators see information in the directory and also control access to that information. The physical and logical layers are completely separate.

Physical Components

The physical components of Active Directory are sites and subnets. A *site* is a combination of one or more IP subnets connected by highly reliable links. A *subnet* is a group of network IP addresses. You use sites and subnets to create a directory structure that mirrors the physical structure of your organization.

You use sites to map your network's physical structure. As shown in Figure 8, a site typically has the same boundaries as your local area networks (LANs). Because site mappings are separate and independent from logical components in the directory, there's no necessary relationship between your network's physical structures and the logical structures in the directory.

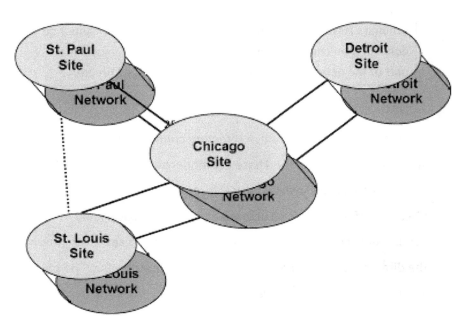

Figure 8 Mapping sites to network structure.

Whereas sites can be associated with multiple IP address ranges, each subnet has a specific IP address range. Subnet names are shown in the form *network/bits-masked*, such as 10.1.11.0/24. Here, the network address 10.1.11.0 and network mask 255.255.255.0 are combined to create the subnet name 10.1.11.0/24. Figure 9 shows the related subnets for several LANs. Each LAN is associated with two subnets. For example, the St. Paul network is associated with the 10.1.11.0/24 subnet and the 10.1.12.0/24 subnet.

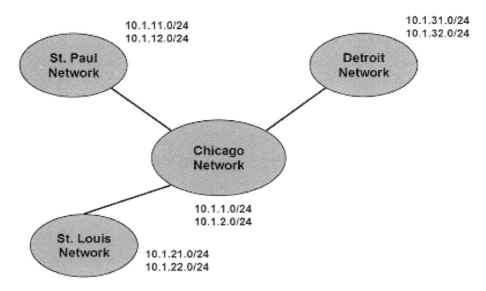

Figure 9 LANs within a WAN and their related subnets.

Ideally, when you group subnets into sites, you should ensure that all subnets are well connected. *Well connected* means that the subnets are connected by reliable, fast connections. Generally, fast network connections are at least 512 kilobits per second (Kbps). To also be reliable, the network connections must always be active, and there must be available bandwidth for directory communications above the normal network traffic load.

In Figure 10, the Detroit and St. Louis networks are connected to the Chicago network using a 512 Kbps connection and therefore are considered to be well connected. Because of this, all three networks can be part of the same site. On the other hand, the St. Paul network is connected to the Chicago network with a 256 Kbps connection and to the St. Louis network with a 128 Kbps connection. Because of this, the

St. Paul network is not considered well connected and should not be part of a site that includes the other networks.

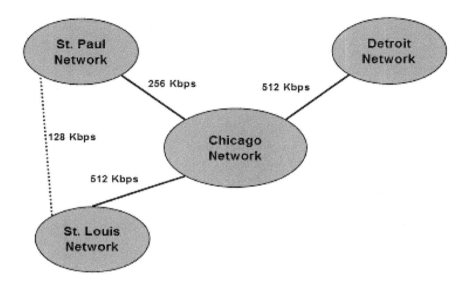

Figure 10 LANs within a WAN and the related connection speeds.

When you browse Active Directory, you see the logical components rather than the physical components. The reason for this is that sites and subnets are not part of the normal Active Directory namespace. Sites contain only computer objects and connection objects. These objects are used to configure replication between sites. Computers are assigned to sites based on their location in a subnet or a set of subnets.

As an administrator, you must create sites and subnets as appropriate for your organization. You must place domain controllers within sites to optimize authentication and replication.

Logical Components

The logical components of Active Directory are domains, domain trees, domain forests, and organizational units (OUs). These components help you organize resources in a logical structure. This logical structure is what is presented to users.

Domains

Domains are logical groupings of objects that share common directory databases. In the directory, domains are represented as container objects. Within a domain, you can create accounts for users, groups, and computers as well as for shared resources such as printers and folders.

In Figure 11, a domain object is represented by a large triangle, and the objects it contains are shown within it.

A domain can store millions of objects and is the parent object of all objects it stores. Keep in mind, however, that a domain stores information only about the objects it contains and that access to domain objects is controlled by security permissions. The security permissions assigned to an object determine which users can gain access to an object and what type of access any particular user has.

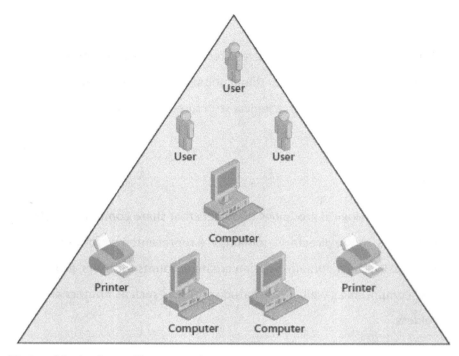

Figure 11 An Active Directory domain.

The directory can contain one domain or many domains. Each domain name must be unique. If the domain is part of a private network, the name assigned to a new domain must not conflict with any existing domain name on the private network. If the domain is part of the public Internet, the name assigned to a new domain must not conflict with any existing domain name throughout the Internet. Because of this, you must register public domain names through a designated registrar before using them. You can find a current list of designated registrars at InterNIC (*http://www.internic.net*).

Because a domain can span more than one physical location, a domain can span one or more sites. A single site also can include resources from multiple domains. Each domain has its own security policies and settings.

Domain functions are limited and controlled by the domain functional level. Several domain functional levels are available, including the following:

- **Windows Server 2003**   Supports domain controllers running Windows Server 2003, Windows Server 2008, Windows Server 2008 R2 and later.
- **Windows Server 2008**   Supports domain controllers running Windows Server 2008, Windows Server 2008 R2 and later.
- **Windows Server 2008 R2**   Supports domain controllers running Windows Server 2008 R2 and later.
- **Windows Server 2012**   Supports domain controllers running Windows Server 2012 and later.
- **Windows Server 2012 R2**   Supports domain controllers running Windows Server 2012 R2 and later.

You set the domain functional level when you install the first domain controller in a new domain. Although you can raise the domain functional level, you cannot lower the domain functional level.

Trees

Although domains are important building blocks for implementing Active Directory structures, they are not the only building blocks. Other important building blocks are domain trees. *Domain trees* are logical groupings of domains.

> **Note**   Within the directory, the tree structure represents a
> hierarchy of objects, showing the parent-child relationships
> between the objects. The domain at the top of the tree is the root
> domain. The root domain is the first domain created in a new
> directory tree, and it is the parent of all other domains for that
> particular domain tree. Other domains that you create in the
> domain tree are child domains.

As an administrator, you create domain trees to reflect your organization's structure. Domains in a tree share a contiguous namespace. The domain name of a child domain is the relative name of the child name appended to the name of the parent domain.

In Figure 12, imaginedlands.com is the parent of tech.imaginedlands.com and sales.imaginedlands.com. The tech.imaginedlands.com domain has related subdomains: eng.tech.imaginedlands.com and dev.tech.imaginedlands.com. This makes tech.imaginedlands.com the parent of the child domains eng.tech.imaginedlands.com and dev.tech.imaginedlands.com.

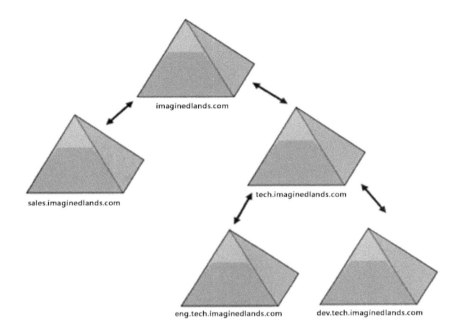

Figure 12 A domain tree.

Forests

Domain forests are logical groups of domain trees. Domain trees in a
domain forest are separate and independent. As such, domain trees
that are members of a forest do not share a contiguous namespace. In
fact, when you add a new domain to Active Directory that is part of a
different namespace, the domain is added as part of a new tree in the
forest. For example, if Active Directory has a single tree as shown in
Figure 12, and you add the domain reagentpress.com to the directory,
the domain is added as part of a new tree in the forest, as shown in
Figure 13. This domain becomes the root domain for the new tree.

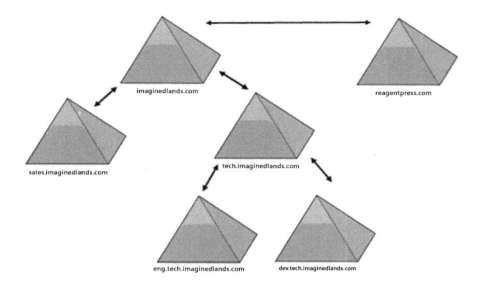

Figure 13 A domain forest with two domain trees.

As an administrator, you create domain forests to reflect your organization's structure. Domains in a forest operate independently but share a common schema. The forest enables communication across member domains. Like domain trees, domain forests have root domains. The first domain created in a new forest is the forest root domain. The first domain created in any additional tree within the forest is the root domain only for the additional tree. In Figure 14, imaginedlands.com and reagentpress.com are the root domains for their respective domain trees, but because cpanld.com was the first root domain created, it is the forest root domain.

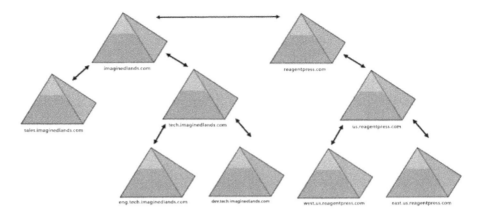

Figure 14 An extended domain environment.

> **Tip** Domains in a forest are connected through implicit two-way transitive trusts. A trust is a link between two domains in which one domain (referred to as the *trusting domain*) honors the logon authentication of another domain (referred to as the *trusted domain*). Trusts join parent and child domains in the same domain tree and join the roots of domain trees. The default protocol used for trusts is Kerberos version 5.

Forest functions are limited and controlled by the forest functional level. Several forest functional levels are available, including:

▪ **Windows Server 2003** Supports domain controllers running Windows Server 2003 and later. When all domains within a forest are operating in this mode, you see improvements in both global catalog replication and replication efficiency for Active Directory data. Because link values are replicated, you might see improved intersite replication as well. You can deactivate schema class objects and attributes; use dynamic auxiliary classes; rename domains; and create one-way, two-way, and transitive forest trusts.

▪ **Windows Server 2008** Supports domain controllers running Windows Server 2008 and later. When all domains within a forest are operating in this mode, you see improvements in both intersite and intrasite replication throughout the organization. Domain controllers can use Distributed File System (DFS) rather than File Replication Service (FRS) for replication as well. Further, Windows Server 2008 security principals are not created until the primary domain controller (PDC) emulator operations master in the forest root domain is running Windows Server 2008. This requirement is similar to the Windows Server 2003 requirement.

- **Windows Server 2008 R2**   Supports domain controllers running Windows Server 2008 R2 and later. When a forest is operating at this level and using domain controllers running Windows Server 2008 R2 and later, domain controllers support several functionality and performance enhancements specific to the R2 release, including Deleted Object Recovery, Managed Service Accounts, and Offline Domain Join.

- **Windows Server 2012**   Supports domain controllers running Windows Server 2012 or later. When a forest is operating at this level and using domain controllers running Windows Server 2012 and later, domain controllers are able to use the many functionality and schema improvements provided. Kerberos with Armoring requires updating schema for Windows Server 2012 but does not require this forest functional level.

- **Windows Server 2012 R2**   Supports domain controllers running Windows Server 2012 R2. When a forest is operating at this level and using domain controllers running Windows Server 2012 R2 and later, domain controllers are able to use the functionality and schema improvements provided, including authentication policies and protected users mode.

Organizational Units

Organizational units (OUs) are logical containers used to organize objects within a domain. Because OUs are the smallest scope to which you can delegate authority, you can use OUs to help manage administration of accounts for users, groups, and computers and for administration of other resources such as printers and shared folders.

By adding OUs to other OUs, you can create a hierarchy within a domain. Because every domain in a domain forest has its own OU hierarchy, the OU hierarchy of a domain is independent from that of other domains.

Ideally, you create OUs to make administration easier. You can use OUs to:

- Reflect the way resources and accounts are managed.
- Reflect the department structure within the organization.
- Reflect the geographic locations for business units.
- Reflect cost centers within the organization.

Following this, you might create OUs for each division or business unit within the organization. This would allow you to delegate authority to unit-level administrators who would have permissions to manage accounts and resources only within a particular business unit. If a unit-level administrator later needs permissions in another business unit, you can grant the administrator the appropriate permissions for the additional OU.

By default, all child OUs inherit permissions from parent OUs. Because of this, an administrator who has permissions for a parent OU can also manage the accounts and resources of any child OUs of that parent. For example, if North America is the parent OU and the child OUs are United States and Canada, an administrator who has permissions for North America would by default also have permissions for United States and Canada.

In Figure 15, the imaginedlands.com domain uses the organization of a sales and services company with global operations in North America, Europe, and South America. Sales and Services are top-level OUs. Sales has three nested OUs: NA, Europe, and SA. Services has three nested OUs: NA, Europe, and SA. In this environment, administrators can have several levels of responsibility.

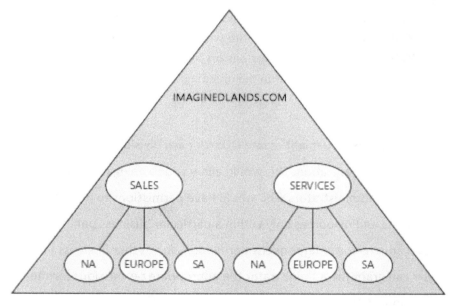

Figure 15 Organizational units within a domain.

Domain administrators have permissions for the domain and all OUs. Administrators for the Sales OU have permissions for the Sales OU and its nested OUs but do not have permissions for the domain, the Services OU, or any OUs nested within the Services OU. Within the Sales OU, subadministrators for NA, Europe, or SA have permissions only for that OU.

4. Managing Active Directory

Administrators spend a lot of time managing Active Directory. I discuss basic tools and techniques in this section.

Working with Active Directory

When you establish domains and forests by installing domain controllers, Active Directory creates default user accounts and groups to help you manage the directory and configure access controls. Important default users and groups include:

- **Administrator**   A default user account with domainwide access and privileges. By default, the Administrator account for a domain is a member of these groups: Administrators, Domain Admins, Domain Users, Enterprise Admins, Group Policy Creator Owners, and Schema Admins.
- **Administrators**   A local group that provides full administrative access to an individual computer or a single domain, depending on its location. Because this group has complete access, you should be very careful about adding users to it. To make someone an administrator for a local computer or domain, all you need to do is make that person a

member of this group. Only members of the Administrators group can modify this account. Default members of this group include Administrator, Domain Admins, and Enterprise Admins.

- **Domain Admins**   A global group designed to help you administer all the computers in a domain. Members of this group have administrative control over all computers in a domain because they are members of the Administrators group by default. To make someone an administrator for a domain, make that person a member of this group.

- **Enterprise Admins**   A global or universal group designed to help you administer all the computers in a domain tree or forest. Members of this group have administrative control over all computers in the enterprise because the group is a member of the Administrators group by default. To make someone an administrator for the enterprise, make that person a member of this group.

- **Group Policy Creator Owners**   A global group designed to help you administer group policies. Members of this group have administrative control over Group Policy.

- **Schema Admins**   A global group designed to help you administer Active Directory schema. Members of this group have administrative control over schema.

Whenever you work with Active Directory, be sure that you are using a user account that is a member of the appropriate group or groups.

Active Directory Administration Tools

You can manage Active Directory by using both graphical administration tools and command-line tools. The graphical tools are the easiest to work with, but if you master the command-line tools, you will often be able to accomplish tasks more quickly. When you use the command-line tools with the Task Scheduler, you might even be able to automate routine tasks.

Graphical Administration Tools

The graphical administration tools for working with Active Directory are provided as snap-ins for the Microsoft Management Console (MMC). You can access these tools directly on the Administrative Tools menu or add them to any updateable MMC. If you're using another computer with access to a Windows Server domain, the tools won't be available until you install them. One technique for installing these tools is to use the Add Feature Wizard.

Graphical tools you can use to manage Active Directory include:

■ **Active Directory Domains And Trusts**   Used to manage and maintain domains, domain trees, and domain forests. See Figure 16.

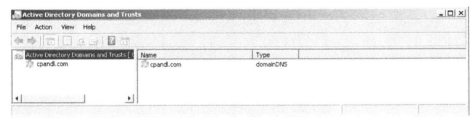

FIGURE 16 Active Directory Domains And Trusts.

■ **Active Directory Sites And Services**   Used to manage and maintain sites and subnets. See Figure 17.

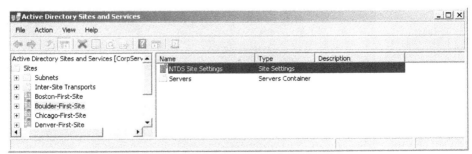

FIGURE 17 Active Directory Sites And Services.

- **Active Directory Users And Computers**   Used to manage and maintain accounts for users, groups, and computers. Also used to manage and maintain OUs. See Figure 18.

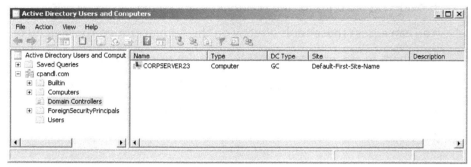

FIGURE 18 Active Directory Users And Computers.

- **Active Directory Schema**   Used to view and manage the schema in Active Directory. You work with object classes and attributes separately. See Figure 19.

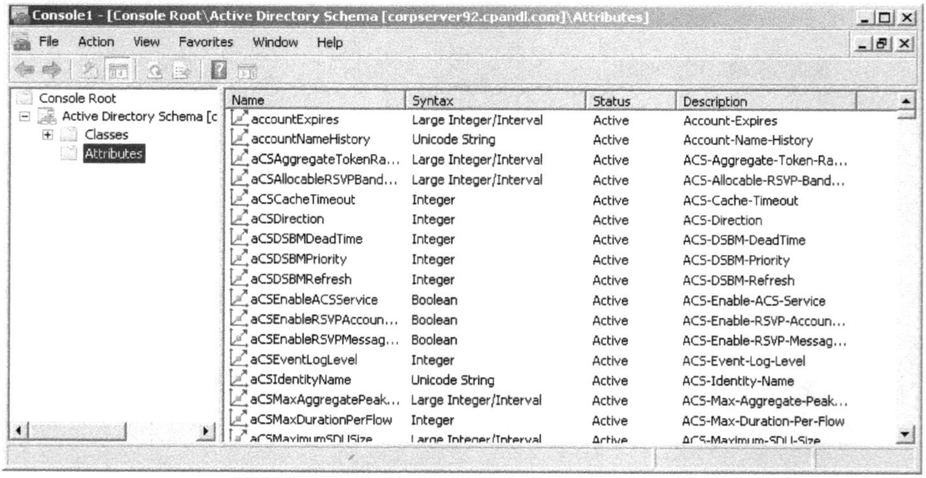

FIGURE 19 Active Directory Schema.

- **ADSI Edit**   Used to edit the ADSI (Active Directory Service Interfaces). This low-level editor lets you manipulate objects and their attributes directly. See Figure 20.

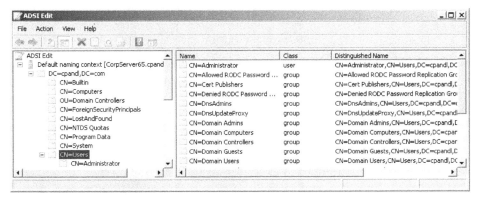

FIGURE 20 ADSI Edit.

Windows Server 2008 R2 and later include Active Directory Administrative Center. Active Directory Administrative Center allows you to perform common Active Directory administrative tasks using an integrated console. Behind the scenes, the console uses PowerShell cmdlets to handle the administrative tasks. The same cmdlets that the console uses are available for your use at a Windows PowerShell prompt.

Although each tool has a different purpose, you can perform some common editing tasks using similar techniques. You can:

- Drag resources to new locations by selecting the objects you want to move and then pressing and holding down the left mouse button while moving the mouse.
- Edit and set properties of multiple resources by selecting the objects you want to work with, right-clicking, and then selecting the operation, such as Add To Group, Disable Account, or Properties.
- Select a series of resources at once by holding down the Shift key, selecting the first object, and then clicking the last object.

- Select multiple resources individually by holding down the Ctrl key and then clicking the left mouse button on each object you want to select.

> **Tip** Windows Firewall can affect remote administration with some MMC tools. If Windows Firewall is enabled on a remote computer and you receive an error message stating that you don't have appropriate rights, the network path isn't found, or access is denied, you might need to configure an exception on the remote computer for incoming Transmission Control Protocol (TCP) port 445. To resolve this problem, you can enable the Windows Firewall: Allow Remote Administration Exception policy setting within Computer Configuration\Administrative Templates\Network\Network Connections\Windows Firewall\Domain Profile. For more information, see Microsoft Knowledge Base Article 840634
> (*http://support.microsoft.com/default.aspx?scid=kb;en-us;840634*).

Command-Line Tools

You also can manage Active Directory from the command line. Command-line tools you can use include:

- **ADPREP**   Used to prepare a forest or domain for installation of domain controllers. Use **adprep /forestprep** and **adprep /domainprep** to prepare a forest or a domain, respectively. Use **adprep /domainprep /gpprep** to prepare Group Policy for the domain.
- **DSADD**   Used to add computers, contacts, groups, organizational units, and users to Active Directory. Type **dsadd objectname /?** at the command line to display Help information on using the command, such as **dsadd computer /?**.
- **DSGET**   Used to display properties of computers, contacts, groups, organizational units, users, sites, subnets, and servers registered in

Active Directory. Type **dsget objectname /?** at the command line to display Help information on using the command, such as **dsget subnet /?**.

▪ **DSMOD**   Used to modify properties of computers, contacts, groups, organizational units, users, and servers that already exist in Active Directory. Type **dsmod objectname /?** at the command line to display Help information on using the command, such as **dsmod server /?**.

▪ **DSMOVE**   Used to move a single object to a new location within a single domain or to rename the object without moving it. Type **dsmove /?** at the command line to display Help information on using the command.

▪ **DSQUERY**   Used to find computers, contacts, groups, organizational units, users, sites, subnets, and servers in Active Directory using search criteria. Type **dsquery /?** at the command line to display Help information on using the command.

▪ **DSRM**   Used to remove objects from Active Directory. Type **dsrm /?** at the command line to display Help information on using the command.

▪ **NETDOM**   Used to manage domain and trust relationships from the command line.

▪ **NTDSUTIL**   Used to view site, domain, and server information; manage operations masters; and perform database maintenance of Active Directory. Type **ntdsutil /?** at the command line to display Help information on using the command.

▪ **REPADMIN**   Used to manage and monitor replication using the command line.

5. Preparing for Active Directory Installation

Preparing for your Active Directory implementation or modification is essential. When you are adding domain controllers to install a new forest, domain tree, or domain, there are some initial decisions you'll have to make. The same is true when you are adding or removing domain controllers within existing domain structures.

Working with Directory Containers and Partitions

In the Active Directory database, stored data is represented logically using objects. Every object in the directory has a name relative to the parent container in which it is stored. This relative name, which is simply the name of the object, is referred to as an object's common name (CN) and is stored as an attribute of the object. Because this name must be unique for the container in which it is located, no two objects in a container can have the same common name. However, two objects in different containers could have the same common name. In this case, the CN of the two objects would be the same within their respective domains, but the complete name in the directory would be different. Why? Because in addition to a common name, directory objects also have a distinguished name (DN).

An object's DN describes the object's place in the directory tree, from the highest container of which it is a member to the lowest. As the name implies, DNs are used to distinguish like-named objects. No two objects in the directory can have the same distinguished name.

The root of the directory tree is referred to as the rootDSE. The rootDSE represents the top of the logical namespace for a directory. Although the rootDSE itself has no parent, all other objects in the directory have a parent. Because it specifically relates to the domain controller on which the directory is stored, the rootDSE will have a slightly different representation on each domain controller in a domain. Below the rootDSE, every directory tree has a root domain. The root domain is the first domain created in a forest and is also referred to as the forest root domain. After you establish the forest root domain, the root never changes, even if you add new trees to the forest.

When you install Active Directory on the first domain controller in a new forest, three containers are created below the rootDSE:

- Forest Root Domain container, which is the container for the objects in the forest root domain
- Configuration container, which is the container for the default configuration and all policy information
- Schema container, which is the container for all objects, classes, attributes, and syntaxes

Active Directory uses object names to group objects into logical categories that can be managed and replicated as appropriate. The largest logical category is a directory partition. All directory partitions are created as instances of the domainDNS object class. The Forest Root Domain container, the Configuration container, and the Schema container each exist in separate Active Directory partitions.

Within Active Directory, domains themselves are simply containers of objects that are logically partitioned from other container objects.

When you create a new domain in Active Directory, you create a new container object in the directory tree, and that container is in turn contained by a domain directory partition for the purposes of management and replication.

Logically apportioning data using partitions simplifies the process of distributing forestwide, domainwide, and application-specific data. Forestwide data is replicated to every domain controller in a forest. Domainwide data is replicated to every domain controller in a particular domain. Application-specific data is replicated to domain controllers that maintain a particular application partition. For example, when you integrate Active Directory with Domain Name System (DNS), domain controllers that are also DNS servers will have the default application partitions used with your DNS zones.

When you need to make changes to Active Directory, you can do so on any domain controller, and you can rely on the Active Directory built-in replication engine to replicate the changes to other domain controllers as appropriate. You can do this because every domain controller deployed in the organization is autonomous, with its own copy of the directory.

At a minimum, every domain controller stores:

- The domain directory partition for the domain of which it is a member
- The schema partition for the forest of which it is a member
- The configuration partition for the forest of which it is a member

Data in a domain directory partition is replicated to every domain controller in the domain as a writable replica. Forestwide data partitions are replicated to every domain controller in the forest. The configuration partition is replicated as a writable replica. The schema partition is replicated as a read-only replica, and the only writable replica is stored on a domain controller that is designated as having the schema operations master role. Other operations master roles are defined as well.

In addition to full replicas that are distributed within domains, Active Directory distributes partial replicas of every domain in the forest to special domain controllers designated as global catalog servers. The partial replicas stored on global catalog servers contain information on every object in the forest and are used to facilitate searches and queries for objects in the forest. Because only a subset of an object's attributes is stored, the amount of data replicated to and maintained by a global catalog server is significantly smaller than the total size of all object data stored in all the domains in the forest.

Establishing or Modifying Your Directory Infrastructure

You install new forests, domain trees, and domains by installing domain controllers in the desired namespace. Whether you are planning to establish or modify your organization's Active Directory infrastructure, there are some initial decisions you'll have to make. The same is true when you are adding or removing domain controllers within existing domain structures. Start by reviewing your organization's Active Directory infrastructure plan with regard to:

- Forests and domains
- Organizational units (OUs)
- Sites and subnets

Regarding forests and domains, it is important to keep in mind how trusts work. A trust is a link between two domains, in which one domain (referred to as the trusting domain) honors the logon authentication of another domain (referred to as the trusted domain). Within a forest, two-way, implicit trusts join parent and child domains in the same domain tree and join the roots of domain trees. Between forests, no default trusts exist. Every forest is separate and distinct from every other forest by default, and you must explicitly establish trusts between forests.

You'll want to try to limit your Active Directory infrastructure to one forest. Otherwise, you'll have to maintain multiple schemas, configuration containers, global catalogs, and trusts, and users will have additional required steps when working with the directory. However, you might need multiple forests when your organization has autonomous business units; when you need to isolate the schema, configuration container, or global catalog; or when there is a need to limit the scope of trust relationships within the organization. For example, you might want the members of your research and development unit to be able to access resources in other business units but not want to allow anyone outside the research and development unit to access its resources.

In some situations, you might not have control over whether your organization has multiple forests. For example, as the result of a merger or acquisition, your organization might gain one or more new forests. In this case, you'll probably need to configure the forests to work with each other by establishing the appropriate trust relationships between the forests.

With multiple forests, you no longer have a single top-level unit for sharing and managing resources. You have separate structures that are autonomous and isolated from one another. By default, forests do not share schema, configuration information, trusts, global catalogs, or forestwide administrators.

You can join forests using cross-forest trusts. Unlike interforest trusts, which are two way and transitive by default, cross-forest trusts are either two way or one way. With a two-way trust, users in either forest have access to resources in the other forest. With a one-way trust, users in one forest have access to resources in the other forest but not vice versa.

When you're establishing a new forest, the first domain you install becomes the forest root domain. The forest root domain can be either a nondedicated root or a dedicated root. A nondedicated root is used as a normal part of the directory. It has user and group accounts associated with it and is used to assign access to resources. A dedicated root, also referred to as an *empty root,* is used as a placeholder to establish the directory base. No user or group accounts are associated with it other than accounts created when the forest root is installed and accounts that are needed to manage the forest. Because no additional user or group accounts are associated with it, a dedicated root domain is not used to assign access to resources.

When you plan to have multiple domains, using a dedicated root domain makes sense. An empty root is easier to manage than a root domain that contains user accounts and resources. It allows you to separate the root domain from the rest of the forest. This is important because the forest root domain cannot be replaced. If the root domain is destroyed and cannot be recovered, you must re-create the entire forest.

> **Tip** The forest root domain contains the forestwide administrator accounts (Enterprise Admins and Schema Admins) and the forestwide operations masters (domain naming master and schema master). It must be available when users log on to domains other than their home domain and when users access resources in other domains.

Within a forest, you define a domain hierarchy by determining the number of domain trees, designating tree root domains, and defining the hierarchy of any required subdomains. You name domains by assigning a DNS name to the forest root domain of each forest, to the tree root domain of each tree, and to each remaining subdomain. Once you create a domain and establish a new namespace, you cannot easily restructure or rename it.

> **Real World** Using the Domain Rename utility (Rendom.exe), which is now included with Windows Server, you can rename domains. However, you cannot use the Domain Rename utility to change which domain is the forest root domain. Although you *can*

> change the name of the forest root domain so that it is no longer
> the forest root logically, the domain remains the forest root
> domain physically in Active Directory.

Before adding a domain tree or child domain to an existing forest, you'll want to consider the increased overhead and hardware costs. The reason for using multiple domains should not be based solely on the number of users, groups, and other objects. Although the number of objects is a factor to consider from a manageability standpoint, a single domain can have millions of objects.

To ensure availability and allow for disaster recovery, every domain should have two or more domain controllers. Some reasons you might want to create additional domains are to:

- Establish distinct namespaces.
- Optimize replication traffic.
- Meet special security or administrative requirements.

Regardless of whether your forest uses a single namespace or multiple namespaces, additional domains in the same forest have the following characteristics:

- **Share common forestwide administrators**   All domains in the forest have the same top-level administrators: Enterprise Admins, who are the only administrators with forestwide privileges; and Schema Admins, who are the only administrators with the right to modify the schema.
- **Share a common global catalog**   All domains in the forest have the same global catalog, and it stores a partial replica of all objects in the forest.

- **Share a common trust configuration** All domains in the forest are configured to trust all the other domains in the forest, and the trust is two way and transitive.
- **Share a common schema** All domain controllers in the forest have the same schema, and a single schema master is designated for the forest.
- **Share a common configuration directory partition** All domain controllers share the same configuration container, and it stores the default configuration and policy information.

With multiple locations, domain changes need to be replicated to all domain controllers, and geographic separation is often a deciding factor. Primarily, this is because there is less replication traffic between domains than within domains (relatively speaking). Therefore, if business locations are geographically separated, it makes sense to limit the replication traffic between locations if possible, and one way to do this is to create multiple domains.

Even within a single business location, the need to limit replication traffic can be a deciding factor for using multiple domains. For example, a large organization with users in multiple buildings in a campus setting may find that the connection speed between locations isn't adequate, and it may be necessary to use multiple domains to limit replication traffic.

As part of establishing forest and domain structures, you'll also have to determine the placement of DNS servers. To ensure proper name resolution, your Active Directory forest will need to have authoritative DNS servers for each domain. If you allow DNS to be configured automatically when you install Active Directory, the new domain controller is automatically set to meet the DNS requirements for joining Active Directory. However, if you installed DNS manually or if your architecture doesn't allow dynamic DNS updates, you'll need to:

- Ensure the _ldap._tcp.dc._msdcs.*DNSDomainName* (SRV) resource record exists in DNS, where *DNSDomainName* is the DNS name of the Active Directory domain.
- Ensure a host (A) resource record for the DNS name of the domain controllers is specified in the data field of the SRV resource record.

Before you install Active Directory, you should ensure the server has a static IP address. If DNS is already set up and the server won't also act as a DNS server, you'll want to designate preferred and alternate DNS servers. If the domain controller will also act as a DNS server, you can set the preferred DNS server to the local loopback address 127.0.0.1 and remove any alternate DNS server (or allow the setup process to do this for you when you install Active Directory).

After reviewing your organization's forest and domain plans, you should review your organizational unit (OU) plan. Within domains, you use OUs to help manage administration of accounts for users, groups, and computers and for administration of other resources such as printers and shared folders. The result of your planning should be a diagram of OU structures for each domain and a list of user groups in each OU.

In a manner similar to the way you use OUs to group users and resources, you use sites to group computers. However, whereas forests, domains, and OUs are logical groupings, sites are physical groupings. Sites reflect the physical structure of your organization's network and are used to optimize network traffic. You define a site for each LAN or set of LANs connected by a high-speed backbone. Any location that is not well connected or is reachable only by SMTP e-mail should be in its own site.

> **Tip** As you design your sites, you also want to determine how other network resources fit into this architecture. You should design sites with Domain Name System (DNS), Dynamic Host Configuration Protocol (DHCP), Distributed File System (DFS) file shares, certificate authorities, Microsoft Exchange servers, and other essential services in mind. Ideally, you want to configure sites so that client queries for a particular network resource can be answered within the site. If every client query for a network resource has to be sent to a remote site, there could be substantial network traffic between sites, which could be a problem over slow WAN links. However, the ideal configuration isn't always possible or practical, and you'll need to carefully evaluate the placement of each resource separately.

Within sites, you'll want to place domain controllers strategically because the availability of Active Directory depends on the availability of domain controllers. A domain controller must always be available so users can be authenticated. For optimum availability and response time, you'll want to ensure the following:

- Each site has at least one domain controller.
- Each domain has at least two domain controllers.

Because replication between sites occurs over site links, you'll want to ensure site links are configured properly. An effective strategy ensures efficient replication and fault tolerance. If a link to a site is unreliable, intermittent, or saturated, you'll want to consider placing additional domain controllers in the site.

Every domain must have at least one global catalog server. By default, the first domain controller installed in a domain is set as that domain's global catalog server. You can change the global catalog server, and you can designate additional servers as global catalog servers as necessary.

When you are configuring sites, designate global catalog servers as necessary to accommodate forestwide directory searching and to facilitate domain client logons when universal groups are available. When universal groups are available in a domain, a domain controller must be able to locate a global catalog server to process a logon request.

For remote locations, you should determine whether read-only domain controllers (RODCs) are appropriate. Additionally, if the wide area network (WAN) link between the remote site and the hub site is limited, you can use universal group membership caching in the remote site to accommodate the logon needs of users in the site. Do not place the global catalog on a domain controller that hosts the infrastructure operations master role in the domain (unless all domain controllers in the domain are global catalog servers or the forest has only one domain).

Establishing Functional Levels

Functional levels affect the inner workings of Active Directory and are used to enable features that are compatible with the installed server versions of the Windows operating system. Each forest and each domain within a forest can be assigned a functional level.

The functional level for a domain within a forest is referred to as the *domain functional level*. When you set a domain's functional level, the level of functionality applies only to that domain. Other domains in the forest can have a different functional level.

Raising the functional level changes the operating systems that are supported for domain controllers and supported Active Directory features. Generally, you cannot lower the domain functional level after you raise it. However, when you raise the domain functional level to Windows Server 2008 R2 or higher, and the forest functional level is Windows Server 2008 or lower, you have the option of rolling the domain functional level back to Windows Server 2008 or Windows Server 2008 R2. You cannot roll the domain functional level back to Windows Server 2003 or lower.

The functional level for a forest is referred to as the *forest functional level*. Generally, you cannot lower the forest functional level after you raise it. However, when you raise the forest functional level to Windows Server 2012 or higher, you can lower it. If you are using Windows Server 2012 forest functional level, you can lower it to Windows Server 2008 R2. If you are using Windows Server 2012 R2 forest functional level, you can lower it to Windows Server 2012, Windows Server 2008 R2. Additionally, with either scenario, if Active Directory Recycle Bin has not been enabled, you can lower the forest functional level to Windows Server 2008. You cannot roll the domain functional level back to Windows Server 2003 or lower.

Exchange Online

A Quick Start Guide for Exchange Online, Office 365 and Windows Azure!

Smart Brain
Training Solutions

XML

Fast
Start

Smart Brain
Training Solutions

www.ingramcontent.com/pod-product-compliance
Lightning Source LLC
Chambersburg PA
CBHW071032050326

40689CB00014B/3621